Thomas Aigner

Compensation for shock damage, pain and suffering, in case of bereavement for pets

Thomas Aigner

Compensation for shock damage, pain and suffering, in case of bereavement for pets

Intangible damage and interpretation of §§ 1331, 1332a ABGB

ScienciaScripts

Imprint

Any brand names and product names mentioned in this book are subject to trademark, brand or patent protection and are trademarks or registered trademarks of their respective holders. The use of brand names, product names, common names, trade names, product descriptions etc. even without a particular marking in this work is in no way to be construed to mean that such names may be regarded as unrestricted in respect of trademark and brand protection legislation and could thus be used by anyone.

Cover image: www.ingimage.com

This book is a translation from the original published under ISBN 978-3-639-62822-7.

Publisher:
Sciencia Scripts
is a trademark of
Dodo Books Indian Ocean Ltd. and OmniScriptum S.R.L publishing group

120 High Road, East Finchley, London, N2 9ED, United Kingdom
Str. Armeneasca 28/1, office 1, Chisinau MD-2012, Republic of Moldova, Europe
Printed at: see last page
ISBN: 978-620-8-09837-7

Contents

Every day, living beings die or sometimes suffer extremely serious injuries. If this happens through the fault of a third party, the person directly injured may first be entitled to compensation for damages or pain and suffering (see Section 1325 ABGB) or certain claims may be made by the surviving dependants (see Section 1327 ABGB) against the person who caused the injury.

The present work deals with the question of whether and how claims of "third" (close) persons for compensation for pain and suffering - on the one hand due to their own mental injury to health, on the other hand due to the (mere) release of feelings of grief or pity or anxiety - as a result of the death or serious injury of the other (close) living being are to be dogmatically justified. The prerequisites for such claims are examined and the question of the extent to which an intense emotional relationship with the dead or seriously injured living being is significant is also answered.

In the context of this thesis, it is shown in particular that such claims of third parties can arise from the death or serious injury of both humans and animals.[1] References to persons always apply equally to all genders.

---

[1] Parts of the work were also first published in the journal TiRuP 2024/A, 65.

CHAPTER 1

Overview of the state of opinion

Essentially, today's case law initially takes the view that if someone suffers their own illness or damage to health due to the death or serious injury of a close relative[2] or a pet[3] , they may be entitled to compensation for pain and suffering (in accordance with Section 1325 ABGB) (**"grief damage with illness value"**, "shock damage").[4]

In E 2 Ob 79/00g and subsequent E, compensation for pain and suffering was also awarded if the death or most serious injury was not witnessed by the victim, but the (mental) illness or damage to health occurred as a result of (later) notification of an accident. On the other hand, in the case of direct involvement in an accident, pain and suffering compensation was awarded even if there was no relationship of kinship or special closeness.[5]

The justification or examination of careless behaviour is disputed in detail.[6]

However, if there is no physical injury (illness or damage to health) within the

---

[2] ZB 2 Ob 109/19x; 9 Ob 9/22x; 2 Ob 126/23b.

[3] ZB LG Feldkirch 8 Cg 262/96g ZVR 2001/67; LGZ Vienna 12.06.2003, 36 R 174/03k; BG Liesing 03.08.2004, 8 C 785/02g; OLG Vienna 12 R 146/10v ZVR 2012/35. The Supreme Court did not rule on the merits in E 1 Ob 125/16p (dismissal of the appeal on points of law due to the lack of a significant legal issue regarding the authorisation by the guardianship court [Section 62 (1) AuBStrG]). Sa 6 Ob 55/04p (award by the first and second instance, dismissal of the appeal [§ 502 para. 2 ZPO]). AA 10 Ob 3/20v.

[4] Cf. instead of many *Perner/Spitzer/Kodek*, Burgerliches Recht[7] (2022) 342; *Riedler*, Zivilrecht IV Schuldrecht Besonderer Teil - Gesetzliche Schuldverhaltnisse[6] (2022) Rz 3/10. Sa *Danzl/Karner* in KBB7 § 1325 Rz 29; *Hinteregger* in *Kletecka/Schauer,* ABGB-ON[1.06] § 1325 Rz 41; 2 Ob 45/93; 2 Ob 99/95; RIS-Justiz RS0116865. With regard to pets, the doctrine is divided (for example, essentially [in the case of gross negligence] *Beisteiner*, Angehorigenschmerzengeld. Der Ersatz von Schock- und Trauerschaden bei Totung oder Schwerstverletzung naher Angehoriger [2009] 182 ff mwN; in contrast, for example, *Hinteregger* in *Kletecka/Schauer,* ABGB-ON[1.06] § 1325 ABGB Rz 50, who, however, affirms the possibility of compensation for grief pain [see below]).

[5] 2 Ob 120/02i.

[6] See for example *Karner*, Rechtsprechungswende bei Schock- und Fernwirkungsschaden Dritter? ZVR 1998, 182: weighing of interests; in contrast *Reischauer* in *Rummel*[3] § 1325 Rz 5: knowledge of suitability for damage. Sa *Kramer*, Schockschaden mit Krankheitswert - noch offene Fragen? in *Apathy* et al (eds.), Festschrift fur Helmut Koziol zum 70. Geburtstag (2010) 743 (754 ff); 2 Ob 163/06v. The older case law (e.g. 3 Ob 331/50; 2 Ob 6/71) is still different: non-reimbursable third-party damage. Criticism of unlawfulness towards relatives *Schickmair*, Dogmatik des Schmerzengeldrechts, in *Kerschner* (ed.), Schmerzengeld. Commentary and Judicature[2] (2020) Rz 147 ff.

meaning of Section 1325 ABGB, but **merely feelings of grief,**[7] , the **damage** is **exclusively immaterial (non-material)**:

In this regard, the **case law**, which is probably overwhelming, states that immaterial damages (in general) are only to be compensated/compensated if this is expressly stipulated in special statutory provisions.[8] Accordingly, case law initially denied an award of "bereavement pain compensation" in the event that there was mere grief without illness value, because the payment of pain compensation was only provided for by Section 1325 ABGB in the event of personal bodily injury (and the suffering resulting from the loss of loved ones was to be assigned to the general life risk).[9] However, since a change in case law, the Supreme Court has also awarded bereavement damages based on a legal analogy (in particular to Sections 1331, 1328, 1329 ABGB and Section 213a ASVG) if there was an intense emotional bond, as typically exists between next of kin, and on the condition that the death was grossly negligent or intentional.[10] The circle of next of kin has been expanded over time: from parents and children[10][11] to spouses,[12] life companions,[13] siblings - but only if they live in the same household -,[14] and stepchildren.[15] In the case of mourning the death of (pets), however, an award of bereavement damages has so far been rejected in

---

[7] Or, in the case of the most serious injuries, feelings of pity or, especially in the case of life-threatening injuries, feelings of anxiety.

[8] See e.g. 9 Ob 36/00k and many more; RIS-Justiz RS0022544. However, some courts in the 19th century certainly assumed that full satisfaction (§ 1324 ABGB) generally also included compensation for the offence caused within the meaning of § 1323 ABGB (i.e. material compensation for non-material damage suffered) (e.g. OGH 29.04.1886, 4044 GlU 11007; 26.09.1888, 8409 GlU 12365; sa OGH 16.11.1887, 12981 GlU 11837).

[9] IdS for example 3 Ob 331/50; 2 Ob 6/71.

[10] 2 Ob 84/01v; RIS-Justiz RS0115189; RS0115190.

[11] ZB 2 Ob 84/01v; 2 Ob 263/06z.

[12] ZB 2 Ob 62/05i; 8 Ob 98/20z.

[13] ZB 8 Ob 127/02p; sa 2 Ob 212/04x; 2 Ob 15/07f.

[14] ZB 2 Ob 90/05g (here: no household community, but in casu intensive community of feeling could be proven); 2 Ob 55/08i; 4 Ob 176/19i; 10 Ob 41/20g (here: no household community, but cordial and intimate relationship, regular contact, joint holidays; intensive community of feeling could be proven).

[15] However, in E 2 Ob 126/23b, which was recently issued in relation to a stepchild, the Supreme Court only dealt with "shock damage" because the "bereavement pain allowance" was no longer an issue in the appeal proceedings.

one E;[16] on the grounds that non-material damage due to the loss of an animal is covered by Section 1331 ABGB and is only to be compensated in the case of intent, and that the loss of an animal is far removed from grief equivalent to the loss of a person.

In the context of bereavement damages, an E[17] also appears particularly controversial (and should therefore be mentioned here), which, in the case of the (mere) swapping of a newborn child on a maternity ward, awarded compensation for emotional pain suffered based on bereavement damages case law, even though the child neither died nor was injured in any way. The reasoning of the Supreme Court referred - although the contractual circumstances were also correctly analysed - primarily to the case law on bereavement damages (and thus to an analogy with provisions that are applied in particular [also] in cases of tortious damage). In casu, however, it could have been examined more precisely whether and how the respective specific breached contractual obligation (obligation of success or duty of care) was also aimed at the protection of non-material interests (and which exactly). Generally speaking, doubts arise at one point in the e-argumentation:[18] As will be shown below, the dogmatic justification for the award of compensation for grief is also based on an intense emotional relationship: If such a relationship existed with someone who is ultimately killed (or seriously injured), an award of compensation for grief (or pity/anxiety in the case of serious injury) can be considered. In the case in question, an intense emotional bond developed and existed with the child, who was regarded as one's own for more than twenty years and with whom one lived in the same household. Even after such an exchange becomes known, however, the feelings towards the beloved child that was raised will (as a rule) not change. This emotional relationship was not affected by the disclosure of the

---

[16] 2 Ob 142/20a.

[17] 4 Ob 208/17t. See also *Wild/Weichbold*, Die Ersatzfähigkeit ideeller Schaden infolge der Verwechslung von Kindern nach der Geburt. A discussion of the decision of the Supreme Court of 22 March 2018, 4 Ob 208/17t, iFamZ 2018, 272.

[18] See immediately. *Wild/Weichbold*, iFamZ 2018, 272, are also critical of the justification of the E in terms of method and content.

circumstances in casu (as would have been the case if the raised child had been killed). With regard to the biological child, there was (mere) ignorance of its whereabouts/fate; this child could live, it could be well, and there was no indication whatsoever that the contrary could (even) have been feared.[19] The statement made in the E that a non-material impairment of the parents (through the exchange) is comparable in terms of value to a death or serious injury can therefore not be accepted in my opinion.

Opinions on the payment of bereavement damages in general (without specific reference to animals) vary in the **doctrine**. One part of the doctrine assumes that non-material damage is generally to be compensated anyway if the law provides for full satisfaction (and does not stipulate otherwise in special provisions). The "compensation for the offence caused" in Section 1323 ABGB therefore concerns the compensation/compensation of non-material damage.[20] As a result, this approach can be used to argue for the compensation of non-material damage in cases of intent and gross negligence, as Section 1324 ABGB grants the injured party full satisfaction in these cases.[21] This general regulation is extended, excluded or restricted by special provisions (e.g. §§ 1325, 1330, 1331 ABGB).[22]

---

[19] As could have been the case in a violent abduction.

[20] See e.g. *F. Bydlinski*, Der Ersatz ideellen Schaden als sachliches und methodisches Problem (Teil I/II), JBl 1965, 173 (179 ff [there also on the development in the scientific discussion]), 237 (247 f); *Hinteregger* in *Kletecka/Schauer*, ABGB-ON[1.05] § 1324 Rz 3; *Karner*, Der Ersatz ideeller Schaden bei Korperverletzung (1999) 78 f; *dens*, Anmerkung zu OGH 16. 5. 2001, 2 Ob 84/01v, ZVR 2001, 287; see *dens*, Zur Ersatzfahigkeit von Schock- und Trauerschaden - eine Bilanz, in *Huber/Neumayr/Reisinger* (eds.), Festschrift Karl-Heinz Danzl zum 65. Geburtstag (2017) 87 (90); *Koziol*, Haftpflichtrecht I[4] D/3 Rz 10 f; *Wolff* in *Klang* VI[2] 122 f, 152. See also *Danzl/Karner* in KBB[7] § 1323 Rz 3.

[21] *Hinteregger* (in *Kletecka/Schauer*, ABGB-ON[1.05] § 1324 Rz 3; sa *dies*, Trauerschmerzengeld und der Anspruch auf immateriellen Schadenersatz im osterreichischen Recht, in FS Danzl 71 [83 f]), however, on the basis of a comprehensive legal analogy, is also in favour of compensation for non-material damage in cases of slight negligence. *Strasser* (Der immaterielle Schaden im osterreichischen Recht [1964] 35 ff) goes further in his approach, considering immaterial damage to already be covered by the concept of (positive) damage in § 1293 ABGB, so that compensation for slight negligence is therefore also possible in principle (unless the law stipulates otherwise in special provisions on the scope of compensation). See also *Mayer-Maly*, Gedanken zum Ersatz immaterieller Schaden, DRdA 1965, 56.

[22] *Koziol*, Haftpflichtrecht I[4] D/3 Rz 11.

Another part of the doctrine is based in particular on § 16 ABGB and the violation of personal rights.[23] Since there are inherent rights that are already recognisable by reason, everyone must respect appropriately protected personal rights.[24] Via the third-party effect of fundamental rights[25] in conjunction with Section 16 ABGB, constitutionally guaranteed fundamental rights can also acquire inter privatos significance. The relevant part of the doctrine argues: If the fundamental rights applicable to the state also provide for compensation for non-material damage when they are violated by the state, then this must also apply in the area of private law by way of third-party effect.[26] However, even if no separate claim for compensation for non-material damage is provided for in the event of a violation of fundamental rights, liability between private individuals is advocated and based on a violation of the right of personality in accordance with Section 16 ABGB in conjunction with the respective fundamental right (e.g. Art 8 ECHR).[27]

Finally, critical voices in the doctrine deny an award of mere bereavement damages,[28] as all the above-mentioned attempts at justification are considered unsuitable. For example, it is pointed out that "not mourning" is not a legal right protected by the legal system and that such protection from grief is not covered by the protection of personality under Section 16 of the Austrian Civil Code.[29]

The question of compensation for pain and suffering for the loss of animals is rarely addressed in legal doctrine. However, *Hinteregger*[30] critically scrutinises previous case law, according to which compensation for pain and suffering is awarded for mourning the loss of people, but not for mourning the loss of pets:

---

[23] S FN 26 and 27; sa *Beisteiner*, Angehörigenschmerzengeld 79 ff.

[24] Cf. instead of many only *Meissel* in *Fenyves/Kerschner/Vonkilch*, Klang[3] § 16 Rz 48 ff.

[25] See also below in the text at FN 109 ff.

[26] *Reischauer* in *Rummel*[3] § 1329 Rz 8; sa *dens* aaO § 1324 Rz 10: Even slight negligence is sufficient.

[27] *Wagner* in *Schwimann/Kodek*[4] § 1293 Rz 49b ff: encroachment on the right of personality to a close family relationship, liability for gross negligence; see also *Reischauer*, comment on 4 Ob 208/17t, JBl 2018, 660.

[28] ZB *Harrer* in *Schwimann*[3] Anh § 1325 Rz 5 ff.

[29] *Schickmair* in *Kerschner*, Schmerzgeld[2] Rz 178 f.

[30] In *Kletecka/Schauer*, ABGB-ON1.0[6] § 1325 ABGB Rz 50.

The application of the rules for property damage (Section 1331 ABGB) to the death or injury of an animal must be reconsidered because the value that the legal system attaches to animals has changed fundamentally in the meantime. § Section 285a ABGB declares that animals are not property, and Section 1332a ABGB stipulates that the immaterial value of the animal for its owners must also be taken into account for the reasonableness of the treatment costs for an injured pet. "It is therefore only logical to also take into account the immaterial value of an animal in the event of death. In view of the high emotional significance that certain pets (dogs, cats, horses) have for many people today, an award of non-material damages (analogous to bereavement damages) would be entirely justified." *Hinteregger*[31] argues in favour of a restrictive interpretation of Section 1331 ABGB, so that compensation for emotional harm caused by the death of a pet should not be linked to particularly serious fault on the part of the tortfeasor. *Wagner*[32] (also) has massive reservations about an argument according to which the bond with a pet cannot evoke the emotional feeling of grief in the same intense way as the loss of a person. "For many people, pets provide a sense of security and emotional joy that people, partners and society can never convey in this form. The loss of a pet can cause people great grief."

---

[31] In FS Danzl 71 (84).

[32] Comment on 2 Ob 142/20a, IUR Newsletter 4/2021, 10, https://www.jku.at/fileadmin/gruppen/ 147/PDF/Newsletter/IUR-NL_2021-04.pdf (retrieved on 01/06/2024).

CHAPTER 2

Dogmatic classification and justification of bereavement compensation - own opinion

1. Grief with disease value

If the third party in question has an illness or health impairment of their own that has arisen because the injuring party unlawfully and culpably injured or killed another (first injured) person, the third party may (in accordance with the Austrian Civil Code) be entitled to compensation for pain and suffering[33] in accordance with Section 1325 ABGB if they were close to the injured or killed person or were involved in an accident that caused the injury/death.[34]

In my opinion, however, two aspects in particular must be considered: If, for example, a violation of a **protective law** (within the meaning of § 1311 ABGB) took place, which caused the bodily injury or death of the other person, and if the third party's claim for compensation for pain and suffering is based on this violation of the protective law, it must be examined on a case-by-case basis, whether (and from what) the provision in question was also intended to protect the third party who only "indirectly" (e.g. by participating in the accident, including witnessing the accident or as a close relative via later news of the death or serious injury) suffers or develops psychological damage (examination of the **unlawfulness connection**).[35] Such a connection of unlawfulness with

---

[33] Since the suffering of pain as emotional damage/damage to sensation cannot be directly restored to its previous state and thus compensated under tort law, the legal system grants a (different) advantage as "compensation" for the disadvantage of negative feelings/perceptions as a substitution, namely a pecuniary benefit (payment for pain and suffering), so that the injured party should ultimately be able to make himself happy (see only instead of many *Nippel* [Explanation VIII/1, 183] with regard to pain: "....... that the injured party is provided with a better enjoyment of life, a greater sense of well-being, which is in a fair relationship with the discomfort caused by the inflicted pain"; see *Spitzer*, Schadenersatz fur Datenschutzverletzungen. Zugleich Bemerkungen zum Diskussionsstand zum Ersatz ideeller Schaden, OJZ 2019, 629 [632 f]).

[34] S at FN 4. In this context, the term "shock damage" is also sometimes used.

[35] The same applies to any breach of contract. If, for example, obligations arising from a medical treatment contract are breached, the protective purpose of the relevant obligation must be considered in addition to a careful examination of causality. Cf. on the protective purpose of a treatment contract (examination contract) - in casu regarding prenatal diagnostics

regard to "indirect" psychological harm to third parties will probably only very rarely or hardly ever exist, for example, in the case of a violation of statutory provisions of the Road Traffic Act. For the adaquance - which must also be observed here - see below.

If the third party's claim for compensation for pain and suffering is based (in any case) on the **violation of *his* physical integrity** itself (violation of an absolutely protected legal interest), it is more likely to be successful; he is the directly injured party. In this case, the described unlawfulness context will also recede into the background (the existence of the absolutely protected legal interest [of the third party] might naturally protect the bearer of the legal interest [the third party] from an injury). To this end, two aspects will come into focus in individual cases: the **careless behaviour** (behavioural injustice) **towards the third party** and the adequacy. On the one hand, it is therefore necessary to examine how a *person in a position of moral responsibility* would have behaved *in the situation of the tortfeasor*. According to *Reischauer*[36] , with regard to the breach of duty of care with respect to the occurrence of damage, this means examining whether this reasonable person could have foreseen the possible occurrence of damage (recognisability for the reasonable person ex ante).[37] Psychological damage to a person directly involved in the accident will generally be foreseeable. The situation is therefore fundamentally different with regard to a third party who merely learns of the death or injury of another person (e.g. through news of some traffic accident with whose victims there is no personal relationship whatsoever).[38] In the case of a personal connection, on the other hand, the third party sympathises much more intensely, which is also

---

and damage to assets - also most recently in detail E 3 Ob 9/23d (stronger Senate), in which the Supreme Court excellently and approvingly departs from deviating previous case law, now assesses "wrongful birth" and "wrongful conception" in the same way and correctly arrives at a result (in both cases, liability for maintenance costs arises in the event of corresponding causality) that corresponds to the principles of tort law.

[36] In *Rummel*[3] § 1295 Rz 12a.

[37] Sa *Reischauer* in *Rummel*[3] § 1325 Rz 5.

[38] *Reischauer* in *Rummel*[3] § 1325 Rz 5: not attributable to the causer as a breach of due diligence.

foreseeable for a reasonable person.

On the other hand, in the context of **adequacy** (according to objective criteria), it will have to be examined whether the occurrence of such damage to the third party as a result of such merely "indirect" behaviour (via the death/injury of another person's body) affecting the psyche of the third party is still within the scope of *general life experience* or whether an atypical causal process occurred. Pre-existing mental illnesses or rare circumstances in the "mental environment" with an extremely low tolerance for sad news should also not be overlooked. This leads, among other things, to the subject area of the damage and to questions of superseding/hypothetical (or, depending on the situation of the case, added) causality.[39] Apart from this, extreme (outside the range of fluctuation of the psyche given by general life experience) psychological damage can cause[40] a lack of adequacy. If, for example, the psyche of the third party is indirectly affected by a mere minor physical injury to another person (e.g. a "minor scratch" on the skin), the issue of adaquacy will be particularly relevant and should generally be denied.[41]

In some case law and literature, formulations are sometimes used according to which the risk of an unreasonable extension of liability is limited by the fact that a particularly strong reason for attribution is required, i.e. the act of infringement must appear to the third party to be highly likely to cause shock damage; or that the shock must be understandable with regard to the cause in order to prevent an extension of liability. From a dogmatic point of view (however), the **"prevention of an extension of liability"** per se does not constitute a separate additional requirement for damages; in particular if (as is also expressly stated in case law) the direct damage to the third party within the meaning of Section 1325 ABGB is taken as a basis. Rather, according to general principles, the examination of the specific careless behaviour and the adequacy test represent

---

[39] See on the whole only *Reischauer* in *Rummel*[3] § 1302 Rz 13a ff mwN.

[40] Cf *Beisteiner*, Angehorigenschmerzengeld 222 f.

[41] Unless (as described above) the lack of due diligence towards the third party is already denied anyway.

the relevant limitations of shock compensation.

It is also necessary to examine whether there has been careless behaviour or whether it is still within the scope of general life experience if the (psychological) damage occurs precisely to such a third person; think, for example, of notified relatives who have had no contact with the injured or deceased person for decades - in this case, a claim will regularly fail. In the case of **persons who directly witness an accident themselves,**[42] or **persons who are close to the (seriously) injured or deceased person (i.e. are emotionally connected to them)** and learn of the injury or death (e.g. close relatives, spouses, registered partners, partners, partners,[43] and persons living in the same household[44] or best friends[45]), harm within the meaning of Section 1325 ABGB will generally be foreseeable for a reasonable person and - if causality exists - will generally not be outside the realm of general life experience.

If all requirements under tort law are met, **compensation for pain and suffering** is to be paid in application of **Section 1325 ABGB even in the case of slightly negligent damage**. If (however) gross negligence or intent is present, compensation for mere grief may also be considered,[46] whereby the case law

---

[42] See 2 Ob 208/23m mwN. A close personal relationship is not necessary (see for example *Karner* in FS Danzl 87 [94]; sa *dens* aaO 108 f with regard to the question of any contributory negligence of the first injured party).

[43] This refers to people in a (romantic) relationship based on partnership, which is not reflected in a shared flat/household or a material economic community, but in which a deep emotional community and the feeling of togetherness as partners is in the foreground. Sa FN 87.

[44] On emotional relationships within patchwork families (keywords: "social parenthood", "social siblings") see jungst *Schoditsch*, Die schadenersatzrechtliche "Kernfamilie" im Licht des Art 8 MRK, OJZ 2024, 283 (285).

[45] This refers to best friends with whom - in individual cases, demonstrably - a special emotional relationship exists (however, most recently 2 Ob 208/23m [in casu, however, award of compensation for pain and suffering due to witnessing the accident]). With regard to the argumentation of the Supreme Court that a purely friendly relationship is not anchored in the legal system, it should be noted that both for foreseeability in the assessment of negligent behaviour and in the context of adequacy, a legal anchoring is not important; emotional attachment exists independently of this. In the adaquacy test, for example, it is only relevant whether, according to general life experience, there can be a strong enough emotional relationship with best friends to suffer the respective damage through the death of the best friend.

[46] E.2.

correctly takes an increase into account as part of the overall assessment.[47]

2. Grief without disease value

It is now questionable whether or not compensation for the exclusively immaterial damage is available in those cases in which there is no illness or damage to health, but merely feelings of grief[48] on the part of the third party. Admittedly, prima vista a claim to compensation for pain and suffering for mere The idea that grief is a feeling that is part of (everyday) life has something to it. However, if the legislator, within the scope of its freedom of design, generally provides for compensation for emotional distress - as non-material damage - in the event of gross negligence[49] or orders compensation for (similar) emotional damage for individual case constellations and an analogous application or a general conclusion seems necessary[49] , then compensation for grief pain and suffering will also have to be awarded accordingly.

a) General compensation for non-material damage

Section 1323 ABGB distinguishes between actual indemnification and full satisfaction, which also includes compensation for loss of profit and repayment of the offence caused. If the damage was caused by malicious intent or conspicuous carelessness, the injured party is entitled to full satisfaction in accordance with **§ 1324 ABGB**, but in other cases only actual compensation[50] .

It follows from the combination of both provisions that **in the case of gross negligence** (intent or gross negligence) **the non-material damage is *generally also to be compensated*[51]** (if all conditions for compensation are met). Accordingly, this view was expressed in some older cases, for example, that the

---

[47] See only 1 Ob 114/16w; 8 Ob 98/20z; 9 Ob 9/22x.

[48] Or, in the case of the most serious injuries, feelings of pity or, especially in the case of life-threatening injuries, feelings of anxiety.

[50] [49] E.2.d).

[51] [50] For full satisfaction, see also *Nippel*, Erlauterung VIII/1, 184 ff.

[52] [51] It is therefore a question of the redemption of the offence caused within the meaning of § 1323 ABGB, of material compensation for the non-material damage suffered; see FN 33 and *Zeiller*, Commentar III/2, 757.

full satisfaction (Section 1324 ABGB) generally also includes the redemption of the offence caused within the meaning of Section 1323 ABGB[52] . A large part of the doctrine -[49] E.2.a). also considers immaterial damage to be eligible for compensation in this sense if there is gross negligence.[54]

If this means that in general - in the case of gross negligence or wilful intent - non-material damage must also be compensated, the question arises as to what happens with **special provisions** in which the legislator explicitly addresses non-material damage. Such norms can often be seen as an extension or restriction of the general basic rule (example of extension: § 1325 ABGB: Compensation for pain and suffering must be paid even in cases of slight negligence; example of restriction: § 1330 ABGB: according to the prevailing view, no compensation for immaterial damage). If there is no departure from the basic rule of Sections 1323 et seq. of the Austrian Civil Code (ABGB) in the case of a special provision, but its content is essentially merely repeated, the possibility of a statutory clarification should also be considered in view of the current case law, which requires an express order for compensation for non-material damage.

b) Special legal provisions

Anyone who assumes (as is the case law prevalent today) that immaterial damages are not already compensable in general or always in the case of gross negligence - because they are already covered by the general concept of damages[53] or by full satisfaction[54] - is faced with the question of whether there are any gaps in the system of individual express provisions on compensation for immaterial damages that are contrary to plan and require analogous application;

---

[53] [52] ZB OGH 29.04.1886, 4044 GlU 11007; 26.09.1888, 8409 GlU 12365; sa OGH 16.11.1887, 12981 GlU 11837. Other more recent E: see e.g. 9 Ob 36/00k; RIS-Justiz RS0022544.

55[53] S *Strasser* above in FN 21.

56[54] E.2.a).

or whether a broad conclusion can be drawn from individual provisions[55] .

Compensation for non-material damage is addressed in detail or advocated by reference: with regard to compensation for pain and suffering as a result of bodily injury, e.g. in Section 1325 ABGB, -[54] S e.g. FN 20.

c) In particular § 1331 ABGB

§ Section 1331 ABGB stipulates that anyone who suffers damage to their property intentionally or through the conspicuous carelessness of another person is also entitled to claim the loss of profit and, if the damage was caused by an act prohibited by a criminal law or out of malice and malicious intent, the value of the special preference[56] .[57] The compensation of the special preference concerns a non-material damage ("affection interest").[58] It is often stated in the literature that compensation for the special preference requires a "particularly qualified fault" (namely either criminal behaviour or wantonness and malice [which sometimes seems to mean a particularly qualified intent]).[59]

With regard to the **conduct subject to criminal law**, it can sometimes be described as a dispute as to whether negligent behaviour is also sufficient if the criminal offence is (exceptionally) already fulfilled in the case of negligence.[60]

57[55] See also E.2.c) and E.2.d).

58   [56] 11 AtomHG, § 13 EKHG, § 176 ForstG, § 79h GTG, § 162 LFG, § 163 MinroG, § 14 PHG, § 3 RHPflG; with regard to compensation for other immaterial damage, e.g. in §§ 1328, 1328a, 1331 ABGB, § 29 DSG, §§ 6 ff MedienG, § 8 MRG, § 12 PRG, § 87 UrhG, § 16 UWG.

[57] In the case of slight negligence, compensation pursuant to § 1332 ABGB is based on the fair market value (cf. § 305 ABGB; on the inclusion of usability in the asset value *Holzner* in Rummel/Lukas[4] § 305 Rz 2; 8 Ob 41/22w).

[58] It is about special feelings that are associated with the object (such as a memento); sa 1 Ob 163/18d (no emotional attachment to a hedge whose function as a privacy screen was temporarily reduced).

[59] See, for example, *Danzl/Karner* in KBB[7] § 1331 Rz 1 (here "particularly qualified fault" is understood to mean malice and malicious intent and is contrasted with behaviour under criminal law); *Harrer/Wagner* in *Schwimann/Kodek*[4] § 1331 Rz 1 (here there is also talk of a further differentiation of the structured concept of damage by § 1331 ABGB); *Hinteregger* in *Kletecka/Schauer*, ABGB-ON[1.06] § 1331 Rz 5; *Reischauer* in *Rummel*[3] § 1331 Rz 1 aE.

[60] This is probably the prevailing view: see for example *Reischauer* in *Rummel*[3] § 1331 Rz 3; *Wolff* in *Klang* VI[2] 166; 1 Ob 160/98f; see also *Huber* in *Fenyves/Kerschner/Vonkilch*, Klang[3] § 1331 Rz 18 f.

In E 1 Ob 160/98f, according to the Supreme Court, no punishable negligent act was evident *in casu*, but the Supreme Court did assume that the existence of a punishable negligent act according to § 1331 ABGB was sufficient. In all cases, it is important that criminal law must sanction the damage to property as such.[61]

In the more recent literature, it is sometimes pointed out that **malice aforethought and schadenfreude** must be cumulative and that a precise distinction between the two terms is not possible anyway;[62] sometimes no interpretation or definition of these terms is even attempted. Other authors, however, argue in favour of an alternative linking of malice and schadenfreude.[63] According to *Geroldinger*[64] , in the case of malice aforethought, it is about the pleasure in the destruction or the action itself that leads to it; in the case of schadenfreude, on the other hand, it is precisely about the harm done to the victim as a result of the damage. In both constellations, the reason for the exacerbation of liability is an idealised gain. According to *Reischauer*[65] , someone acts out of malice if the damage is done out of pleasure in the damage (*Reischauer* refers to an E from 1905[66]); Schadenfreude is understood as the pleasure in the other person's feeling of discomfort, which is supposed to result from the damage[67] . In the older literature, the interpretation of the two terms "wantonness" and "schadenfreude" is given a much broader scope: *Wolff*, for example, [68] speaks of wantonness in the case of pleasure in the damaging behaviour and its immediate consequences, without thinking of the further consequences. In particular, the wilful person does not think about the

---

[61] *Reischauer* in *Rummel*³ § 1331 Rz 3 mwN.

[62] *Harrer/Wagner* in *Schwimann/Kodek*⁴ § 1331 Rz 4.

[63] ZB *Geroldinger*, Der mutwillige Rechtsstreit (2017) 152 ff; *Hasenohrl*, Das oesterreichische Obligationenrecht II² (1899) 158; *Spielbuchler* in *Rummel'* § 305 Rz 4.

[64] See also *dens*, loc. cit. 58 ff on the highly diverse meanings of the term "wilfulness" in common parlance and in various historical legal provisions; the term was understood differently and in a wide range, from the proximity to particular malice to particular recklessness.

[65] In *Rummel*³ § 1331 Rz 4.

[66] Supreme Court 14 June 1905, 7793 GlUNF 3089.

[68] [67] *Reischauer* in *Rummel*³ § 1331 Rz 5.

[69] [68] In *Klang* VI² 166.

feeling of displeasure of the injured party caused by the damage or does not act with due care. Wilfulness does not even always have to be intentional, because pleasure is the predominant motive; if the person acting is so absorbed by the idea of the pleasure-inducing effect that he does not think about an unlawful result at all, does not even imagine it or does imagine it but does not grasp its significance, he is acting negligently. *Wolff* understands schadenfreude as a feeling of pleasure at the unpleasantness caused to the other person by the damage. In *Stubenrauch*[69] , causing harm out of schadenfreude is described as being done with the intention of gloating over the pain of the person harmed; it is done out of wilfulness, merely to gratify one's whim[70] . *Hasenohrl*[71] explains that the motive for the act is generally the same for the question of damages, but that there is an exception to this: If the motive consists of wantonness or schadenfreude, i.e. if the perpetrator did not intend to derive any advantage from the commission of the act, but only acted out of reckless pleasure in the success of the act or out of malicious pleasure in the disadvantage caused to another, this entails stricter treatment of the tortfeasor according to § 1331 ABGB. In this respect, a distinction must be made between two types of malicious intent: simple malicious intent and malice aforethought. *Nippel*[72] points out that the value of the particular preference is also to be compensated if the damage inflicted intentionally or out of conspicuous carelessness is of such a nature that it has itself been declared prohibited by an express criminal law or the damage has been inflicted out of malice or glee. In his commentary on § 1331 ABGB, *Zeiller*[73] deals primarily with the loss of profit and, with regard to the price of the special preference, refers mainly to the actions prohibited by criminal law,

---

[70] [69] Commentary II[8] 711.

[71] [70] For the older literature on criminal law in relation to the terms "malice" and "wantonness", see also the notes in *Kadecka*, Bosheit und Mutwille, GZ 1909, 242.

[72] [71] Code of Obligations II[2] 158.

[73] [72] Explanation VIII/1, 211.

[73] Commentary III/2, 767.

but does not address the interpretation of malice and schadenfreude.[74][75]

In order to determine the meaning of the terms and provisions used in § 1331 ABGB, it is essential to take a look at the **history of codification**:

In **Martini's draft**, § 44 of the 13th main section of Part 3 stated: "If damage is intentionally inflicted, whether through self-interest, robbery, theft, theft, fraud, unauthorised violence or through malice and malicious intent, i.e. through the deterioration or destruction of a thing, the damaged party is entitled to claim both the value of his particular preference for the thing and the loss of further profit." This was followed by § 45 with the introductory words: "However, if the damage results from negligence or culpable ignorance, ...".

Section 454 (in the 13th main section) of Part 3 of the **original draft** of the ABGB stated: "If the damage is intentionally inflicted, whether through self-interest, namely through robbery, theft, fraud, unauthorised violence, or through malice and malicious intent, the injured party is entitled to claim both the value of the particular preference for the object and the loss of profit." This was followed by § 455 with the introductory words: "1st but the damage was caused by negligence or culpable ignorance, ...".

It is clear from this that the **intention of the provisions** is (simply) **to** order compensation for the value of the particular preference and the loss of profit **in the event of intent**. It is irrelevant whether the intent is based on self-interest (in this regard, various [criminal] acts are cited as examples) or otherwise (in this regard, wilfulness and malice are cited as examples).

Finally, the text sections were reorganised/reworded in the course of the **revisions**. *Zeiller* [76][76] declares (however) in the deliberations that the text presented at the meeting of 9 June 1806 was consistent (in terms of content) with § 454 of the original draft. This is due to the fact that the purpose of the amendment/rewording was evidently to emphasise compensation for lost profits

---

[74] As will become clear, this was probably due to the fact that *Zeiller* apparently naturally proceeded from a certain understanding of the terms resulting from the history of codification, which did not need to be explained further.

[76] S *Ofner* (ed.), Protocols II 198 f.

and - as the supplement and the ultimately adopted text show[77] - (ultimately) to provide for compensation in cases of gross negligence (and not only in cases of intent). However, this does not change the fact that the value of the particular preference is simply to be replaced in the case of intent - which is why there is also talk of conformity with the original draft. In this respect, therefore, there is **agreement with the original draft and Martini's draft**, from which it is clear what was ultimately meant by the introduction of wilfulness and schadenfreude: namely the indication of **examples of** (other) **intentional acts**, which were specifically mentioned alongside other examples of intent (namely self-interested acts [such as theft, robbery etc]).

The history of codification therefore shows that the historical legislator had in mind intentional damage to property, regardless of whether or not it was prohibited by criminal law, for example. According to the historical intention of the law (which emerged from the drafts and remained the same in the course of revision and final editing), **wantonness and malice** are merely **exemplary designations** for cases which, although they may not appear as separate offences in the Criminal Code, are nevertheless committed as a matter of principle. An important finding of this historical consideration is therefore that (due to the mere exemplary payment) there does not necessarily have to be a punishable act, wilfulness or malicious intent *per se*, but that **generally a (simple) intentional damage is a prerequisite and is sufficient for the value of the particular preference with regard to a thing to be compensated.**

Emphasis: The value of the special preference in accordance with § 1331 ABGB is generally to be (only) recognised in the case of preference:

However, if the offence was actually punishable or was committed with malice or malicious intent, the question still arises as to whether teleological arguments could possibly outweigh the historical understanding (as intentional acts). **On the basis of the heightened lack of value** that the legislator (generally) assumes when it sanctions behaviour under criminal law, or on the basis of the

---

[77] Cf *Ofner* (ed.), Protokolle II 803.

specifically heightened lack of value of wilful damage and damage committed with malice aforethought, it can be assumed that **even in the exceptional cases of punishable negligent behaviour directed against the property**[78] or **negligent behaviour arising from malice aforethought (or malice aforethought)** [79] , liability is aggravated.

d) Analogy and generalisation

After clarifying the interpretation of Section 1331 ABGB, the following can now be stated: Section 1325 ABGB provides for compensation for non-material damage (compensation/compensation for unpleasant [pain] feelings) as a result of damage to one's own physical integrity, whereby even slight negligence is sufficient[80] . § Section 1331 ABGB provides for compensation for non-material damage (compensation/compensation for unpleasant [grief] feelings) as a result of damage to one's own property, whereby in principle intent is generally required (or in special cases negligence is sufficient[81]).

Against this background, an **analogy** can be drawn to these provisions with regard to the compensation of feelings of grief in the event of death (or feelings of compassion/anxiety in the event of serious injury) of a person - if one assumes (like the case law above) that immaterial damages are not to be compensated in general, but on the basis of individual provisions. In particular, the following **general conclusion can** also be **drawn**: If the law provides for compensation for feelings of grief even in relation to an inanimate object, then there must be all the more compensation for (generally more intense) feelings of grief in relation to a living being. Admittedly, it could still be argued that

---

[78] [78] IdS *Reischauer* in *Rummel*[3] § 1331 Rz 3; *Wolff* in *Klang* VI[2] 166; 1 Ob 160/98f; sa FN 61.

[79] [79] IdS *Geroldinger*, Mutwilliger Rechtsstreit 154 f: wilfulness can also be gross and deliberate - particularly intentional - negligence. On Schadenfreude sa *Wolff* in *Klang* VI[2] 166.

[80] [80] See only *Harrer/Wagner* in *Schwimann/Kodek*[4] § 1325 Rz 67.

[81] [81] E.2.c).

according to Section 1331 ABGB there is an ownership relationship to the object, whereas this is of course not the case in relation to the person killed/injured[82] . When § 1331 ABGB speaks of "his property" and stipulates compensation for the particular preference, the legislator obviously had the case in mind that a feeling of attachment to a thing will typically only exist to one's own thing. The essential special idea (however) lies in the emotional bond to itself, namely the ***emotional bond* to a thing**. This idea can be transferred (as a general conclusion) to the ***emotional bond to a*** (foreign) ***living being* (here: human being)**.

In consideration and analogous application of §§ 1325 and 1331 ABGB, according to which, on the one hand, compensation is due for non-material damage in the event of damage to one's own physical integrity, even in cases of slight negligence, and, on the other hand, in the event of damage to an object to which a special emotional bond exists, [83]compensation for non-material damage in the case of intent (only in exceptional cases also in the case of negligence), compensation for feelings of grief as a result of the destruction of the legal right to life (or feelings of compassion/anxiety in the case of the most serious impairment of the legal right to bodily integrity) of another (here: human) living being with whom there is a special emotional bond, may well be in favour of the **requirement of gross negligence (intent or gross negligence)**.[84]

Emphasise: For the allocation of pure mourning money it is a rough precondition

e) Prima facie evidence of the emotional relationship

The remarks already made on **careless behaviour** and **adequacy**[85] also apply

---

[82] [82] See *Schickmair* in *Kerschner*, Schmerzgeld^2 Rz 37.

[83] The legal interests of life and bodily integrity are to be valued more highly than the legal interest of property. This regularly has an impact on the intensity of feelings of pain and grief, which is also expressed in the legal provisions (§§ 1325, 1331 ABGB). At the same time, it should be noted that feelings are generally more intense when one's own legal interests (in particular physical integrity) are violated than when other people's legal interests are violated.

[84] This is also required by case law for the award of bereavement compensation.

[85] E.1.

here when it comes to the question of compensation for pain and suffering as compensation for grief without illness value. On the one hand, this applies to the severity of the injury to the body of the other person and the associated indirect effect on the psyche of the third party. On the other hand, it must be examined whether it was foreseeable for the person in question in the specific situation or whether it is generally still within the scope of general life experience that the damage would occur to such a third person. Both generally apply to third parties who have an intense emotional relationship with the injured or deceased person.

The **special emotional relationship must generally be proven by the injured party** in accordance with the case law[86] . However, for persons living in the same household (e.g.: spouse, registered partner, life partner, child, parent) or persons living in separate households but who are nevertheless typically (usually) closely connected (e.g.: partner,[87] child, parent), a corresponding emotional relationship can generally be assumed in the context of the **prima facie conclusion**[88] . In the case of other persons (e.g.: best friend,[89] separated siblings[90]) with whom there is not typically a very close relationship (but more or less frequent or sporadic contact), the injured party must prove a special emotional relationship in individual cases without using the prima facie inference.

---

[86] See for example 2 Ob 90/05g; 6 Ob 103/19v.

[87] This refers to persons in a (romantic) relationship based on partnership, which (admittedly) is not reflected in a shared home/household or in a material economic community, but in which a deep emotional community and the feeling of togetherness as partners is in the foreground. In addition, with regard to spouses or registered partners, reference should be made to §§ 90 ff ABGB or §§ 8 f EPG and to the possibility of temporary separate living arrangements (cf. for example *Hinteregger* in *Fenyves/Kerschner/Vonkilch*, Klang[3] § 90 Rz 4 ff; *dies*, Familienrecht[10] [2022] 54 ff; *Wagner*, Zivilrecht VI Familienrecht[5] [2022] Rz 7/14 ff, 21/12); with regard to lifelong journeys, the fact that a flexible system between the developed criteria is advocated there anyway (see RIS- Justiz RS0047000).

[88] Also known as prima facieevidence or prima facie evidence: It is a matter of empirical theorems and typical sequences of events (in the case of a typical lack of evidence with regard to negligence or causality). The party bearing the burden of proof proves certain facts from which, according to life experience, other facts can be inferred with considerable probability, for which he bears the burden of proof. Conclusions about a person's inner state may also be admissible as prima facie evidence. See *Koziol*, Haftpflichtrecht II[3] A/5 Rz 108 f; *Reischauer* in *Rummel*[3] § 1296 Rz 4 ff; RIS-Justiz RS0022664.

[89] S FN 45.

[90] S FN 14.

CHAPTER 3

In particular: Bereavement compensation in the event of the death or serious injury of an animal - own opinion

1. Grief with disease value

If the person concerned suffers an illness or damage to health of their own that has arisen because the injuring party unlawfully and culpably injured or killed the animal that was close to the person, the person may be entitled to **compensation for pain and suffering in accordance with Section 1325 ABGB**.[91] The **explanations made under point E.1** apply accordingly.[92] As will be shown **in detail below under point F.2.d)**, the **emotional relationship between a pet owner and his pet**[93] is nowadays generally **just as intense** as the emotional relationship with a child, life companions, etc. Accordingly, it is also **foreseeable** for a reasonable person (when examining careless behaviour) that the pet owner, who has an intense emotional bond with his pet, may suffer emotional damage with a pathological value. The act of severe injury or death is (even) **typically highly likely** to cause emotional damage with disease value.[94] The **death/serious injury of a pet** is (therefore also) **according to (today's) general life experience likely to cause emotional damage with disease value to** the owner (or possibly also to other [reference] persons living in the household).[95] Even in the event of the death/serious injury of an animal that is not a pet, but to which (in individual cases) a special emotional attachment is proven, damage within the meaning of Section 1325 ABGB - if causality exists -

---

[91] See also FN 3.

[92] S there also on the lack of due care and on adequacy. For the (foreseeable and within life experience) occurrence of emotional damage, any legal anchoring of a relationship is also irrelevant here; feelings and emotional damage (with or without disease value) arise independently of a legal anchoring of a relationship.

[93] The term "pet" is used in this paper in the sense of the most commonly used understanding (domesticated animal living/kept in the household) and therefore corresponds most closely to the term "pet" within the meaning of § 4 Z 3 of the Animal Welfare Act.

[94] See also E.1 for high suitability.

[95] See for example OLG Vienna 12 R 146/10v ZVR 2012/35. For the intensity of the emotional relationship between (today's) pet owners and their pets, see F.2.d) in detail.

will generally not be outside the scope of general life experience.[96]

In case law, pain and suffering compensation was awarded for the compensation of grief damage with illness value (shock damage), for example: when the first defendant drove a car backwards and ran over the 14-year-old miniature poodle of the plaintiff with the left rear tyre and seriously injured it, whereby an emergency operation by the veterinarian was unsuccessful, the dog died and the plaintiff suffered a psychological impairment with disease value (experience-reactive maldevelopment with a mentally unstable condition, temporary depression with slight sleep disorders and anxious-phobic behaviour);[97] or, for example, when two of the plaintiff's dogs were bitten by the defendant's dog, whereby one of the plaintiff's two dogs, with which she had an intimate relationship, died a week later due to the injuries and the plaintiff suffered a psychological impairment with disease value (acute stress reaction, subsequent adjustment disorder with nightmares, sleep disorders, anxiety and depression).[98]

2. Grief without disease value

a) General compensation for non-material damage

As described in E.2.a), it can already be assumed that compensation for non-material damage under §§ 1323, 1324 of the Austrian Civil Code (ABGB) is in principle possible in order to justify compensation (the granting of an advantage) for the disadvantage of negative feelings of grief or anxiety/pity. Whether these feelings result from the death/injury of a person with whom there is a special emotional relationship or from the death/injury of an animal with which there is a special emotional relationship is of course irrelevant per se - the emotional harm has ultimately occurred in both cases. As will become apparent under **point F.2.d)**, such negative feelings **typically** occur among pet owners; **according to (today's) general life experience (and to a high degree)**, the **death/serious injury of a pet** is **likely to cause emotional damage without**

---

[96] See also on German law *Straub/Biller-Bomhardt*, Schockschadensersatz bei Verletzung oder Totung eines Tieres, NJW 2021, 118 (121).

[97] LG Feldkirch 8 Cg 262/96g ZVR 2001/67.

[98] OLG Vienna 12 R 146/10v ZVR 2012/35.

disease value to the owner (or possibly also to other persons living in the household).

Since the special statutory provisions dealing with non-material damage can be understood as an extension, restriction, etc.,[99] the only thing that could stand in the way of an award of bereavement damages for the loss of a beloved pet would be the assertion that Section 1331 ABGB entails a restriction with regard to damage to property (compensation for non-material damage in principle only in the case of intent[100]). However, as will be shown later, Section 1331 ABGB originates from a time when not only the overwhelming social feelings towards animals were different, but also the understanding of the legal system in relation to animals was completely different: In addition to the creation of provisions aimed at animal protection (e.g. under public law), Sections 285a and 1332a were introduced into the ABGB. The contents and basic ideas of these provisions, which are described below[101] , also have an impact on compensation for non-material emotional harm. If one assumes general compensation for non-material damage in the event of gross negligence as well as extensions, restrictions, etc. through special provisions, then the basic idea in particular of Section 1332a ABGB[102] in conjunction with the social development[103] leads to the fact that Section 1331 ABGB, which is seen as a restriction, must be teleologically reduced. Emotional damage caused by the death or serious injury of a (domestic) animal with which there is an intense emotional bond cannot therefore be equated with emotional damage caused by the loss of or damage to an inanimate object.[104] Since emotional damage caused by the death or serious injury of an intensely emotionally attached (domestic) animal is not covered by § 1331 ABGB from a teleological perspective, it is not specifically regulated, so that the general compensation for gross negligence as defined by **§§ 1323, 1324**

---

[99] S on this view in chapter D and E.2.a).
[100] E.2.c.
[101] F.2.b), F.2.c) and F.2.f).
[102] F.2.c) and F.2.f).
[103] F.2.d) and F.2.f).
[104] See in detail below under F.2.e).

ABGB applies.[105]

b) Special legal provisions regarding compensation for non-material damage and in relation to animals

As described in point E.2, the following initial constellation applies in principle: Section 1325 ABGB provides for compensation for non-material damage as a result of damage to one's own physical integrity, whereby even slight negligence is sufficient. § Section 1331 ABGB provides for compensation for non-material damage as a result of damage to one's own property, whereby in principle intent is generally required (in special cases, however, negligence is also required).[106] In addition to § 285a ABGB, which states that an animal is not a thing, § 1332a ABGB also applies.[107] The Animal Protection Act in all its facets and the Animal Transport Act are also mentioned, as is Section 2 B-VG Sustainability,[108] and the criminal offence of cruelty to animals. Art 8 ECHR is also cited, which concerns the right to respect for private and family life, which (as part of the personal concept of life) also includes cohabitation with a pet.[109] Via the indirect third-party effect, fundamental rights can also develop significance in the area of private law (in particular in the context of an interpretation in conformity with fundamental rights, in the context of filling a gap or in the concretisation of general clauses). Of course, this applies to contractual clauses (in particular, via the immorality barrier[110]), but also in the

---

[105] On the other hand, those who are not in favour of general compensation for non-material damage in the sense of the above-mentioned case law ultimately arrive at the same result by analogy and general conclusion (see F.2.f)).

[106] E.2.c).

[107] See below under F.2.c).

[108] Cf. also most recently Constitutional Court G 193/2023 mwN: Animal welfare embodies a widely recognised and significant public interest.

[109] *Pletzer*, Once again: Ban on keeping cats and dogs in the form rental agreement? wobl 2013, 249 (252) mwN.

[110] On the ineffectiveness (pursuant to § 879 para. 3 and § 879 para. 1 ABGB) of (various) clauses concerning a ban on keeping pets in rental agreements, see *Muhlehner*, Die Tierhaltung in Bestandsobjekten - Zulassigkeit der Haltung versus vertragliche Beschränkung (2023) (diploma thesis Linz, available at https://epub.jku.at/obvulihs/id/8880297 or urn:nbn:at:at-ubl:1-63847).

area of tort.[111] Finally, § 250 para. 1 no. 4 EO should also be mentioned, which standardises the impoundability of pets (not intended for alienation) to which an emotional bond exists.

c) In particular also § 1332a ABGB

§ Section 1332a ABGB was introduced at the same time as **Section 285a ABGB**, stating that animals are not property. § Section 285a ABGB aims to clarify the difference between animals and property, which is also emphasised by the fact that a separate paragraph was created for this purpose[112] . According to Section 285a ABGB, animals are protected by special laws; the provisions applicable to property are only applicable to animals insofar as there are no deviating regulations. The materials state that, accordingly, the right of ownership may not be exercised at will, but that "animals are under the special protection of the law and ... protective regulations issued in the interests of the animal must be observed[113] ." § Section 285a ABGB is also used to justify the necessity of the legal interest of animal welfare[114] . With regard to § 285a ABGB, the Regional Court of Vienna, for example, held[115] in connection with the division of marital property: "The protective concept underlying § 285a ABGB is aimed at preserving the life and health of animals as well as protecting the emotional relationship between humans and animals ..."; "In the ... Therefore, when allocating a dog, not only the asset value of the dog must be taken into account, but also the emotional attachment of both spouses to the dog and the dog to them[116] ...".

---

[111] Cf. only *Meissel* in *Fenyves/Kerschner/Vonkilch*, Klang³ § 16 Rz 34 ff. Sa § 16 ABGB and in particular above at FN 27.
[112] JAB 497 BlgNR 17. GP 1.

[112] [113] IA 130/A II-2228 BlgNR 17. GP 2; RAB 3447 BlgBR 1.

[113] [114] *Binder*, Sachenrecht (2003) Rz 2/2; *Bohm*, Rechtliche Probleme und Grenzen des tierschutzerischen Aktionismus, in *Harrer/Graf* (Hrsg), Tierschutz und Recht (1994) 47 (48, 55 ff); *Stabentheiner* in *Fenyves/Kerschner/Vonkilch*, Klang³ § 285a Rz 5.

[114] [115] 44 R 645/02g EFSlg 104.963.

[115] [116] See also 1 Ob 254/22t. For (additional) express statutory provisions in inheritance and family law that require the welfare of the animal, de lege ferenda *Bahn*, Das Tier im Familien-

According to **§ 1332a ABGB**, in the event of injury to an animal, the costs actually incurred for healing or attempted healing are also payable if they exceed the value of the animal, insofar as a reasonable animal owner in the position of the injured party would have incurred these costs. The term "healing costs" is to be understood in the same way for an animal as for a human being.[117]

The **purpose** of § 1332a ABGB is to reimburse the costs of treating an injured animal irrespective of its pecuniary value, in particular to take account of the fact that the owner can have a strong emotional relationship with his animal as a living being and in any case usually does with his pet.

§ Section 1332a of the Austrian Civil Code (ABGB) goes back to an **initiative motion**, according to which the following paragraph was to be added to Section 1323 ABGB: "If an animal that is unjustifiable for the owner due to its nature is injured, the costs actually incurred for healing or attempted healing shall be charged even if they exceed the value of the animal."[118] It was only in the **Judiciary Committee** that the phrase "animal which by its nature is unjustifiable for the owner" (meaning animals with which there is usually a closer emotional bond, such as pets[119]) was replaced by "animal". The JAB justifies this by stating that in the case of a farm animal, with which "there is usually no emotional relationship", a responsible pet owner will not spend an amount that exceeds the value of the animal. A reasonable pet owner would give a pet the usual veterinary treatment, but not extraordinary and very cost-intensive surgical procedures.

However, it depends on the particular circumstances of the injured party; in individual cases, it can therefore be assumed that the injured party has an

---

und Erbrecht, TiRuP 2018/A, 63.

[117] *Danzl/Karner* in KBB[7] § 1332a Rz 3; *Huber* in *Fenyves/Kerschner/Vonkilch*, Klang[3] § 1332a Rz 14. This also includes, for example, expenses to prevent deterioration or to alleviate pain as well as costs arising from an increase in needs and for medication or medical aids. Sa 2 Ob 10/91; 6 Ob 177/19a.

[118] IA 130/A II-2228 BlgNR 17. GP 1. It is also stated (IA 130/A II-2228 BlgNR 17. GP 3): "As in § 1325 ABGB, the term injury also includes other damage to health."

[119] IA 130/A II-2228 BlgNR 17. GP 3.

emotional relationship with an animal that is usually only kept as a farm animal.[120] The changes to the wording in the Justice Committee have therefore tended to extend the scope of application further. See below for the main basic idea expressed in both the initiative motion and the JAB.

The statement in the JAB that a **reasonable pet owner** would give a pet standard veterinary treatment, but not *unusual and* very cost-intensive surgical procedures, must probably be understood as meaning that "unusual" means "not medically indicated"; it therefore refers to "treatments" that are superfluous from a medical point of view, e.g. that were merely cosmetic in nature, or that have no effect according to the current state of medical science. Conventional veterinary treatments, on the other hand, include healing, pain relief or restoration, relief or substitution of bodily functions etc[120] . Of course, this also includes - if medically indicated - cost-intensive examinations, operations, etc. *Harrer/Wagner*[121] can therefore also be agreed with when they state that the veterinarian will generally recommend to the animal owner those measures that a reasonable animal owner would initiate.[123] Against the background of the wording and the historical development as well as with special consideration of the purpose of the standard, the view is therefore wrong that (always) certain percentage -[120] JAB 497 BlgNR 17. GP 1 f. limits in relation to the value of the animal or (in the case of animals without value) absolute amounts could be accepted as "threshold values".[122] If at all, such values could at best provide a

---

[121] [120] Sa *Hinteregger* in *Kletecka/Schauer*, ABGB-ON[1.06] § 1332a Rz 3: Treatment costs, costs for medication, medical aids and transport.

[122] [121] In *Schwimann/Kodek*[4] § 1332a Rz 3. *Harrer/Wagner* (loc. cit.) also point out that the authoritativeness of the responsible animal owner in § 1332a ABGB does not mean a new legally relevant statement, because the duty to minimise damages is violated anyway in the case of excessive expenses.

[122] However, *Huber* in *Fenyves/Kerschner/Vonkilch*, Klang[3] § 1332a Rz 29 f; *Wittwer* in *Schwimann/Neumayr*, ABGB-TK[5] § 1332a Rz 3. In contrast, the Supreme Court (10 Ob 29/16m; in casu even against the background of the question of the proportionality of an improvement under warranty law): "In the case of pets that are not farm animals ... the emotional relationship is usually open ....As far as   the amount of the costs is concerned, the costs
of the usual veterinary treatments a guideline ....of strict adherence to a

rough guide for "farm animals" with which there is no particular emotional relationship[123] . In the case of pets, on the other hand, with which there is a strong emotional bond, the reimbursement of the costs of medical treatment is based (not on values or arbitrarily assumed amount limits, but) - in accordance with the standard purpose of restoring as best as possible the health of the emotionally bonded beloved animal that has been impaired by the damaging party - on the **medical indication**. As described above, a sensible pet owner would have medically indicated treatments or measures carried out in order to heal their beloved pet, alleviate pain, improve their state of health (or prevent deterioration), restore, facilitate or substitute bodily functions, etc. It should also be noted that a sensible pet owner complies with the public law requirements for the protection of the life and well-being of animals.[124] A responsible animal owner will generally not consult several veterinarians at the same time - unless necessary[125] - but will consult a (medically indicated) specialised veterinary clinic (with or without further referral by a [general] veterinarian[126]).

A multiple of the market value as an upper limit ... is precluded by the fact that there are animals with no monetary value at all." See also *Danzl/Karner* in KBB7 § 1332a Rz 3; *Hinteregger* in *Kletecka/Schauer*, ABGB-ON[1.06] § 1332a Rz 2.

[123] [123] Incidentally, a pet owner who has sufficient financial means is to be assumed (*Huber* in *Fenyves/Kerschner/Vonkilch*, Klang[3] § 1332a Rz 25).

[124] See in detail 6 Ob 66/22g, inter alia with reference to §§ 6, 13, 15 Animal Welfare Act. See also *Huber*, comment on 6 Ob 177/19a, ZVR 2021, 398 (399).

[125] Sa *Harrer/Wagner* in *Schwimann/Kodek*[4] § 1332a Rz 3 with reference to BG Melk 01.02.2006, 5 C 2336/04p: If the state of health of a dog does not improve even after several visits to a veterinarian, the consultation of a second veterinarian is (very well) appropriate.

[126] It should also be noted that the standard of care set out in Section 1299 ABGB applies to veterinary treatment (2 Ob 281/04v; 9 Ob 72/06p; 7 Ob 163/13s). If it is apparent to a (general) veterinarian that he does not have the necessary skills of a specialised veterinarian, he must in any case make this clear. See *Aigner*, Gedanken zur Sachverstandigenhaftung, OJZ 2017, 494, on this complex of topics, on the interpretation of Section 1299 and on fault in the assumption of liability. In this regard, it should be mentioned in parenthesis that *Koziol* (Haftpflichtrecht II[3] A/6 Rz 4) apparently misunderstood my explanations in OJZ 2017, 494. I never claimed a differentiation between contractual and tortious liability with regard to the necessary fault of assumption. The initial presentation from the respective perspective (*Aigner*, loc. cit. 496-498) served exclusively to clarify and justify in more detail the increased standard of care brought about by § 1299. A possible exoneration due to a lack of fault of assumption (i.e. in the case of prior acts without fault; see only the repeated citation of the various prior acts from the contractual and tortious area [*Aigner*, loc. cit. 498 f]) is (however) of course possible in both contractual and tortious relationships (see in detail

It is quite clear from the materials to § 1332a ABGB[127] and the purpose of the provision as described above what its **basic idea** is: the **different treatment of living animals on the one hand and inanimate objects on the other** also in **tort law**, especially due to the fact that (unlike with an inanimate [fungible] object) there is usually a **strong emotional relationship with a pet**.

Emphae § 1332aABGB deals with the replacement of emotonally connected tyres in contrast to the replacement in the case of the occupation of leHoer counterparts.

d) Social development / development of intensive emotional relationships

From **times long past**, the relationship between humans and animals is largely/often[128] described with little emotion: Animals served in particular as a source of food or as farm animals. Other domestic animals living in the house or on the farm, such as dogs or cats, often served a practical purpose (e.g. guarding, looking after other animals, hunting mice, etc.). In aristocratic and wealthier households, animals were sometimes regarded as a status symbol.

In the up-and-coming urban bourgeoisie of the **19th century**, more and more pets were kept that did not fulfil any of the tasks described above.[129] They were now kept more for pleasure, whether as well-trained dogs for walking in public or as cushion dogs in private. The changed view was also expressed in art, for example when paintings depicted cats playing or dogs (with or without owners) - sometimes romanticised - in various living situations. Along with increased financial capability, it was now possible to keep pets for pleasure purposes

---

Aigner, loc. cit. 498 f with further references).

[127] IA 130/A II-2228 BlgNR 17. GP 2 f; JAB 497 BlgNR 17. GP 1 f.

[128] There were, of course, exceptions that became publicly known (such as dogs of rulers from different eras that were immortalised in paintings).

[129] This went hand in hand with the displacement of farm animals from urban public spaces, including the outsourcing and mechanisation of the killing of slaughter animals in their own (increasingly industrialised) slaughterhouses. S *Darmann*, Pets and animal lovers. Uber Nahe und Ferne von Menschen und Tieren, in *Krason/Willmitzer* (eds.), Tierisch beste Freunde. Uber Haustiere und ihre Menschen (2017) 12 (40 f).

only.[130]

Pet ownership increased rapidly in the **second half of the 20th century**. In the process, and especially in recent decades, **the emotional significance of pets for people** has **grown steadily**.[131] The pet became a friend and a companion that also accompanies people on an emotional level. The term "companion animal" also emerged to characterise a more modern human-animal relationship, as this was seen as a clearer expression of the quality of the bond between owner and animal than the term "pet".[132]

The number of pets continues to grow in the **21st century**.[133] On an emotional level, pets are now increasingly becoming **equal members of the family**. In the family member concept, hardly any human area remains closed to the animal family member.[134] In **recent years** in particular, the emotional significance and connection between humans and pets has become even stronger.[135]

The **effects** of having a pet are of a psychological and physical nature:[136] On **a psychological level**, the effects range from stimulation of empathy, communication and interaction[137] to reduction of stress,[138] fear and anxiety with

---

[130] In this context, the English term "pet" also developed, the semantic spectrum of which "oscillates somewhere between pet, favourite animal and stuffed animal and comes quite close to the characterisation of a toy" (*Wischermann*, Zwischen "Vieh" und "Freund". Historische Annaherungen an das Selbst eines Tieres, in *Krason/Willmitzer* 49 [61 f]).

[131] Sa *Hinteregger* in FS Danzl 71 (84); *Kitchenham*, Tierisch beste Freunde. Love knows no boundaries (2021) 13 ff. See also *Tuma-Koch*, Die Sonderstellung von Tieren im Zivilrecht (2021) 30 ff.

[132] *Wischermann* in *Krason/Willmitzer* 49 (62 f) mwN.

[133] S about https://www.ots.at/presseaussendung/OTS_20220928_OTS0110/heimtierstudie-in- every-second-household-has-a-pet-picture (published in 2022, accessed on 01/06/2024). See also the international comparison of the keeping of different animals in 2016 https://www.gfk.com/de/insights/haustiere-im-internationalen-vergleich (accessed on 01/06/2024).

[134] *Wischermann* in *Krason/Willmitzer* 49 (63).

[135] Sat below.

[136] For the psychological and physical effects of the relationship with (domestic) animals, see *Julius/Beetz/Kotrschal/Turner/Uvnas-Moberg*, Bindung zu Tieren. Psychologische und neurobiologische Grundlagen tiergestutzter Interventionen (2014) 53 ff mwN; *Kitchenham*, Tierisch beste Freunde 41 ff, 176-188 mwN.

[137] *Julius/Beetz/Kotrschal/Turner/Uvnas-Moberg*, Bindung zu Tieren 65 ff, 69 f; *Kitchenham*, Tierisch beste Freunde 41 ff, 50 ff, 81, 184 ff. See also, for example, *Wischermann* in *Krason/Willmitzer* 49 (75 ff).

[138] *Kitchenham*, Animal Best Friends 174-178.

a demand for (inner) calm,[139] increased trust and trustworthiness,[140] positive mood and reduction of depressive states[141] and possibly improved pain management[142] through to reduction of aggression.[143] **Physiological effects** include (health-enhancing) effects on the cardiovascular system, blood pressure, heart rate, skin temperature, etc.[144] In addition to effects on the immune system, hormonal effects are also associated with living with a pet (e.g. with regard to cortisol, epinephrine, norepinephrine).[145]

Of particular note is the release of the hormone **oxytocin** (also known as **the "bonding hormone"**, "mother-child hormone", "cuddle hormone", etc.), which is associated with feelings of love, trust and happiness. For example, tender touching of newborns causes a release of the hormone, as does a deep look into the eyes; this applies to human children as well as animals and continues in adulthood (in intimate relationships).[146] Stroking dogs or cats leads to an increase in oxytocin levels in both humans and dogs or cats; the same happens with intensive eye contact.[147] The same applies to auditory[148] and olfactory stimuli.[149] *Julius/Beetz/Kotrschal/Turner/Uvnas-Moberg*[150] state: "In fact, the endocrine and physiological effects measured in nursing mothers and their babies are similar to those observed in female dog owners and their dogs after these women had stroked their dogs." Since studies have also shown that the increase in oxytocin levels was higher when subjects petted their own dog (rather than someone else's), this suggests that the increase in oxytocin is

---

[139] *Julius/Beetz/Kotrschal/Turner/Uvnas-Moberg*, Attachment to animals 70 ff.

[140] *Julius/Beetz/Kotrschal/Turner/Uvnas-Moberg*, Attachment to animals 72 f.

[141] *Julius/Beetz/Kotrschal/Turner/Uvnas-Moberg*, Attachment to animals 73 f.

[142] *Julius/Beetz/Kotrschal/Turner/Uvnas-Moberg*, Attachment to animals 75.

[143] *Julius/Beetz/Kotrschal/Turner/Uvnas-Moberg*, Attachment to animals 75.

[144] *Julius/Beetz/Kotrschal/Turner/Uvnas-Moberg*, Attachment to animals 76 ff. Sa *Kitchenham*, Animal best friends 177 f.

[145] *Julius/Beetz/Kotrschal/Turner/Uvnas-Moberg*, Attachment to animals 80 f.

[146] See only *Julius/Beetz/Kotrschal/Turner/Uvnas-Moberg*, Bindung zu Tieren 81, 83 ff, 135 ff, 164 ff, 177 ff; *Kitchenham*, Tierisch beste Freunde 37 ff.

[147] *Kitchenham*, Animal Best Friends 43-45.

[148] E.g. familiar voice, purring etc.

[149] *Julius/Beetz/Kotrschal/Turner/Uvnas-Moberg*, Attachment to animals 92.

[150] Attachment to animals 178.

dependent on the quality of the relationship between humans and animals.[151] The effects of oxytocin are diverse and manifest themselves in many ways on a physiological and psychological level. To summarise briefly, it reduces stress[152], anxiety, relaxation, feelings of trust and well-being, care and a deeper bond[153]. A high level of oxytocin promotes behaviours, emotional states and social cognitions that are of central importance for attachment development; whereby the oxytocin-induced effects are also associated with the attachment figure via the mechanism of classical conditioning[154].

The **emotional bond with the pet** is **also visibly** expressed in **behaviour towards the outside world**; not only during the pet's lifetime in a variety of ways (care in every respect[155], striving for physical closeness and touch [cuddling, stroking etc], intensive communication with the animal ,[156]

---

[151] *Julius/Beetz/Kotrschal/Turner/Uvnas-Moberg*, Bindung zu Tieren 104. Sa *dies*, loc. cit. 105: "Physical contact ... as well as the bond with the animal seem to play the same central role [with regard to oxytocin, author's note] as in the interpersonal sphere ... . It can therefore be assumed that the same mechanisms can be effective in good human-animal relationships, as described in detail ... described in detail using the example of the mother-child relationship."

[154] [152] Physiological effects include a reduction in stress hormones, lower blood pressure, etc.

[155] [153] *Julius/Beetz/Kotrschal/Turner/Uvnas-Moberg*, Attachment to animals 87 ff, 135 ff.

[156] [154] *Julius/Beetz/Kotrschal/Turner/Uvnas-Moberg*, Bindung zu Tieren 150 ff. Sa *dies*, ibid. 180: "The studies presented here provide the first empirical evidence that close human-animal relationships are characterised by the same endocrine regulatory patterns that are characteristic of secure interpersonal attachment and flexible care behaviour towards other humans."

[157] [155] On fostering behaviour sa *Julius/Beetz/Kotrschal/Turner/Uvnas-Moberg*, Attachment to animals 170 ff.

[158] [156] Of course, this takes place not only via word-related or melodic language or other vocalisation, but also in a variety of ways, e.g. via body language, eye contact and facial expressions. For the (respective) significance of facial expressions in communication between humans and animals (and between different species), see *Kitchenham*, Tierisch beste Freunde 41 ff, 50 ff, 81. For these and many other forms of non-verbal communication and interaction, see *Mahr*, Tiergestutzte Interventionen. Integration von Tieren in stationaren Kinder- und Jugendhilfeeinrichtungen in Osterreich (2023) 19 ff (Master's thesis Graz, available at https://unipub.uni-graz.at/urn/urn:nbn:at:at-ubg:1- 187742 or urn:nbn:at:at-ubg:1-187742).

[159] See also *Wischermann* in *Krason/Willmitzer* 49 (63 f).
[160] https://www.sueddeutsche.de/leben/tiere-tierbestattungen-werden-immer-beliebter-dpa.urn- newsml-dpa-com-20090101-200212-99-881824 (accessed on 01/06/2024). Sa

comprehensive medical care, special food selection, toy selection, gifts for holidays and much more), but also when the beloved pet dies.[159] For example, in the form of (steadily increasing annual[160]) pet burials (be it in the form of cremations in pet crematoriums with the urn handed over or urn/earth burials in pet cemeteries) or obituaries in various media and much more. In 2004, an obituary placed in a Swiss daily newspaper for a deceased cat was one of the first of its kind to cause astonishment, whereas today obituaries concerning the death of a pet are commonplace and taken for granted.[161]

As can be seen both in the physiological and psychological effects described and in behaviour, **the emotional bond or emotional relationship that is established with the pet is no different from that with children, companions, etc.**[162] As already indicated, the emotional relationship is also based on reciprocity: the pet also has an emotional bond with the human pet owner, which has the aforementioned psychological and physical effects (and is also accompanied by a corresponding release of hormones [e.g. in relation to oxytocin] on a physiological level).[163]

In 2020, *Schmitt/Kunzmann* published the results of a project carried out between **2017** and **2019** at the University of Veterinary Medicine Hanover on the question of how people deal with death and mourning for their pets. In addition to various essays and other materials, collected quotes from pet owners from the questionnaires were also reproduced.[157] Instead of many, here are just a few examples from the quotes:[158] "I have buried a lot of people, my brother

---

Benkel, Das Mensch-Tier-Verhältnis: Spielräume einer Sozialpartnerschaft, in *Schmitt/Kunzmann* (eds.), Nicht nur dein Tier stirbt. Geschichten und Forschungen zur Trauer um Haustiere (2020) 66 ff.[161] S *Wischermann* in *Krason/Willmitzer* 49 (86 f) mwN.

[162] Cf. also *Wischermann* in *Krason/Willmitzer* 49 (82 f): "Humans and animals establish relationships that are not simple substitutes, but unique. The animal achieves equivalence without language, comparable to the status of sucklings."
See in detail above including the respective Nw; also *Kitchenham*, Tierisch beste Freunde 43 ff, 178-188, 220 ff.

[157] *Schmitt/Kunzmann* (eds.), Tier stirbt 33 ff, 52 ff, 76 ff, 110 ff, 130 ff, 160 ff, 184 ff.
[158] *Schmitt/Kunzmann* (eds.), Tier stirbt 78 ff, 85, 112 f, 118 f.
[166] https://de.statista.com/statistik/daten/studie/1167139/umfrage/verhaeltnis-von-heimtierbesitzern-zu-ihren-haustieren/ (retrieved on 01/06/2024).

when I was 21 years old - he was 19, cancer. That knocked me off my feet. But our dog has simply surpassed everything. It tears you apart. A piece of me has gone with her."; "It hit me just as hard as the death of my son in 2009."; "My husband told me that when I told him now that his father had died, it hadn't hit him as hard as the death of our dog. That sounds harsh and heartless, but I know exactly what he means."; "A pillar of my life has broken away."; "It's a loss of a beloved companion. Whether human or animal, it makes no difference to me - the grieving process is the same."; "The first night I woke up and listened to our dog's breathing until I immediately realised that he was no longer there. My husband wasn't in bed either - he was sitting in the garden on a bench next to our dog's grave, crying."; "I can't go the old rounds. It's too painful. I can think of an incident at every turn. It feels strange to be walking alone in the woods and fields."; "When I write it like this, even after seven years I have a lump in my throat and tears in my eyes."; "I cried for days, weeks, months after his death and I still cry when I write." Overall, the results of the project very often showed how deeply, painfully and persistently grief for the beloved pet was felt.

A study conducted in Germany in **2020** (survey)[166] among pet owners[167] on their relationship with their pets asked about their agreement with various statements from[168] and showed the following result:

▶ "My pet is a member of the family"

> 90% "strongly agree"; 3.9% "somewhat agree"; <u>total:</u> 93.9%

▶ "I treat my pet like my own child"

> 50.6% "strongly agree"; 27.7% "somewhat agree"; <u>total:</u> 78.3%

▶ "For me, my pet comes first"

> 30.9% "strongly agree"; 49.8% "somewhat agree"; <u>total:</u> 80.7%

---

[167] 775 persons.

[168] Selection options: "strongly agree", "somewhat agree", "somewhat disagree", "disagree".

[169] https://de.statista.com/statistik/daten/studie/1336090/umfrage/umfrage-zur-bedeutung-von- haustieren-in-oesterreich/ (accessed on 01/06/2024).

[170] 337 persons.

[171] The question asked was "whether the respective statement applies to your pet or not".

A study conducted in Austria in **2022** (representative survey)[169] among pet owners[170] on the importance of pets asked about agreement with various statements from[171] and showed the following result:

▶ "A pet is like a good friend"

> applies to 94%

▶ "Pets enrich my life"

> applies to 93%

▶ "Losing this pet was going to hit me hard"

> applies to 87%

▶ "Pet pays as a fully-fledged member of the family"

> applies to 82%

A study conducted in Austria in **2023** (representative survey)[159] among pet owners[160] on their life with pets and their purchasing behaviour for pet supplies showed the following result:

▶ For 86%, their animals are part of their family.

Today, animals in general and pets in particular have an exorbitantly higher emotional value than in the past. Many people today opt for pets instead of children or for pets and children in equal measure. The bonds and feelings that are (usually) formed with the respective living creature are completely comparable and intense. Aspects such as **communicating, interacting, developing and showing feelings, seeking physical closeness and touch and the emotional affection between humans and pets are completely comparable and intense, e.g. between humans and children.** Accordingly, **feelings and symptoms of grief are equally intense when a beloved living being dies.**[161]

Emphasis: The emotional bond between a pet owner and his or her pet and the

---

[159] https://www.zza-online.de/branche/branche/article/tierische-familienmitglieder-wie-leben-die-oesterreicher-mit-ihren-heimtieren.html (accessed on 01/06/2024).

[160] 1010 persons.

[161] See e.g. *Gerdes*, Trauer um den Verlust eines Haustieres aus psychosomatisch-psychotherapeutischer Sicht, in *Schmitt/Kunzmann* 124 ff; *Wischermann* in *Krason/Willmitzer* 49 (64). It is about feelings of grief and the pain of separation.

feelings of deafness at the pet's death are just as important today as they were in the past

It is therefore definitely not outside the realm **of general life experience** (according to what has been described in detail in this article so far) that these **intense feelings of grief** occur in the pet owner (or possibly also in other [reference] persons living in the household) **as a result of the death of the pet. Moreover,** this is **also the typical case nowadays**. The act of death is foreseeably **highly likely** to cause the intense feelings of grief described above. The same applies to stressful feelings of pity/anxiety as a result of serious injury.

The emotional bond is otherwise independent of whether the living being with whom the emotional bond was established was conceived by the person concerned: No one would argue that an emotional bond with an adopted child is necessarily less strong simply because it was not conceived by the person; the same applies to an emotional bond with a spouse, companion or pet.

e) Effects on § 1331 ABGB

At the very least, the above explanations with regard to social development and the intensity of the bond and the (grief) feelings that typically occur today as a result of the death or serious injury of the pet kept also show that, **from a teleological perspective, emotional damage caused by the death or serious injury of a pet** is **not** (or no longer) **covered by the "value of the special preference" in Section 1331 ABGB**. In any case, § 1331 ABGB covers the much smaller emotional relationship to an inanimate object, whereby the compensation of such emotional impairment usually only occurs in the case of intent. The very different, namely (today) much higher and more intense emotional relationship of a pet owner to his beloved pet (as an interacting living being that triggers the most intense effects on a psychological and physiological level and leads to a massive emotional bond) does not fit in with this at all. From a teleological perspective, against the background of § 1332a ABGB and the current social significance of (domestic) animals and the intensity of the emotional attachment to pets that exists today[162] , it follows that emotional distress caused by grief due to the death or pity/grief due to the serious injury of a pet (generally speaking: an animal with which there is an intense emotional attachment) is just as little within the direct scope of application of special provisions as emotional distress caused by grief due to the death or pity/grief due to the serious injury of a human being.[163] This means that compensation in application of §§ 1323, 1324 ABGB[164] or, if - like the above-mentioned case law - one does not already assume general compensation for non-material damage, a solution by analogy and general inference is required.

f) Analogy and generalisation

Those who (like the case law above) take the view that immaterial damages are not to be compensated in general, but on the basis of individual provisions, are (again) faced with the question of whether there may be gaps in the system of individual express provisions on compensation for immaterial damages that require analogous application; or whether a general conclusion can be drawn from individual provisions.

As already described in point E.2.d), a **general conclusion** can be drawn **regarding § 1331 ABGB**, as the essential idea behind this provision is the *emotional bond* and even compensation for feelings of grief regarding an **inanimate object** is provided for. This idea can be applied all the more (as a general conclusion) to the more intense *emotional attachment to a living being* **(human or pet[165])**; whereby, according to the legal system, it is self-evident in the case of humans (Section 16 ABGB) and in the case of animals (Section 285a ABGB) that ownership is equally irrelevant, because the intense emotional

---

[162] See F.2.d).

[163] The same therefore applies to emotional distress caused by grief as a result of death or pity/anxiety as a result of serious injury to another ("farm") animal with which - although not typically, as in the case of pets - an intense emotional relationship exists in individual cases, if proven.

[164] F.2.a).

[165] Generally speaking: a person or animal with whom there is an intense emotional bond. Sa F.2.e) on the teleological reduction of Section 1331 ABGB.

attachment to the family dog, for example, exists regardless of whether it is owned by the parents or a child, for example.

Section 1332a ABGB[166] **reflects the different treatment of animals and inanimate objects in tort law**, in that the costs of healing or attempted healing of an animal with which there is usually a strong emotional relationship - regardless of its pecuniary value - are to be compensated. In this way, the law itself expresses the understandable, namely that the *emotional attachment of the animal owner to his (pet) animal* is generally *much higher and more intense than to an inanimate object.*

Added to this is the **social development: animals (and pets in particular)** have an **exorbitantly higher emotional value today than in the past.**[167] Today, pets are **members of the family**. As already discussed in detail, the **feelings that are built up and exist with pets as well as with children, for example,** are **completely comparable and intense**. Aspects such as communicating, interacting, developing and showing feelings, seeking physical closeness and touch and the emotional affection between **humans and pets** are completely comparable and intense, for example between **humans and children**, between **spouses** or **life companions**. This can be seen **in** many ways, **both psychologically and physiologically** (for example with regard to identical hormone release).[168] Accordingly, there are **equally intense feelings of grief when a beloved pet dies** (or feelings of compassion/anxiety when a **pet** is seriously injured).

All in all, the considerations on **analogy and large-scale inference** as in point E.2 result in.d), i.e. **with regard to §§ 1325, 1331** (including the considerations on gross negligence as an expression of a value lying in the middle), in combination with an **analogy to § 1332a ABGB**,[169] **against the background** of

---

[166] See F.2.c) for details.
[167] In detail in F.2.d).
[168] See in detail above under F.2.d).
[169] See above for the essential idea of the provision.

the **other provisions mentioned**[170] and in view of the **social development** and **today's particularly emotional significance of and intensive relationship with pets,**[171] that compensation for grief as a result of the **death of a (domestic) animal** must be **paid** as **a** matter of principle if the death was **intentional or due to gross negligence.** The same applies to compensation for feelings of pity or anxiety as a result of **serious injury to a (domestic) animal** that was caused **intentionally or through gross negligence.**

g) Prima facie evidence of the emotional relationship

As already explained in point E.2.e), to which reference can be made in principle, the special emotional relationship must basically be proven by the injured party.

However, in the case of animals living in the same household (**pets**[172]), a corresponding emotional relationship can generally be assumed as part of the **prima facie conclusion**, as there is typically a particularly strong bond and intense emotional relationship with pets.[173] In the case of **other animals** (e.g. "farm animals" [on a pasture or on a farm in a stable], remotely employed riding horses, etc.) with which there is not typically the closest bond (but more or less frequent or sporadic contact), the injured party would have to prove a special emotional relationship in individual cases without the aid of the prima facie inference.

---

[170] S F.2.b).
[171] F.2.d). Sa F.2.e) on the teleological reduction of Section 1331 ABGB.
[172] FN 93.
[173] S only for F.2.d).

CHAPTER 4

Results

If a person's own **illness or damage to health** results from the fact that the injured party **injures or kills** a **living being (human, animal)** with which there is a **special** (particularly strong) **emotional relationship**, a claim for **compensation for pain and suffering pursuant to Section 1325 ABGB** (even in the case of slight negligence) may be considered, provided that the other requirements for compensation are met. In the case of **direct involvement** in the damaging event (e.g. accident), a special emotional relationship is not relevant.

(Pure) **bereavement compensation** is - if the other conditions for compensation are met - payable **in the event** of **gross negligence** (gross negligence or intent) as compensation for **feelings of grief due to** the **death of a living being (human, animal)** with which there is a **special** (particularly strong) **emotional relationship**.

Similarly, **in the event** of **gross negligence** (gross negligence or wilful intent), **compensation for pain and suffering** is to be paid as compensation for **feelings of compassion or anxiety due to** the **most serious injury to a living being (human, animal)** with which there is a **special** (particularly strong) **emotional relationship**, provided that the other conditions for compensation are met.

The **special** (particularly strong) **emotional relationship** must always be proven by the injured party. For **persons or animals living in the same household** (e.g. spouse, registered partner, pet, child, parent): However, for persons **or animals living in the same household (e.g.** spouse, registered partner, life partner, pet, child, parent) **or** persons **living in separate households who are nevertheless typically strongly connected** (e.g. partner, child, parent), a correspondingly intense emotional relationship can generally be assumed as part of the **prima facie inference**.

In the case of **other persons or animals** (e.g. best friend, separated siblings, distant riding horse) with whom there is not typically a very close relationship (but more or less frequent or sporadic contact), the injured party must prove a special emotional relationship in the individual case (without using the prima facie conclusion).

Bibliography

Aigner, Thoughts on the liability of experts, OJZ 2017, 494.

Apathy/Bollenberger/P. Bydlinski/Iro/Karner/Karollus (eds.), Festschrift fur Helmut Koziol zum 70. Geburtstag (2010).

Bahn, The animal in family and inheritance law, TiRuP 2018/A, 63.

Beisteiner, Relatives' pain and suffering compensation. The compensation of shock and grief damages in the event of the death or serious injury of close relatives (2009).

Benkel, Das Mensch-Tier-Verhaltnis: Spielraume einer Sozialpartnerschaft, in *Schmitt/Kunzmann* 66.

Binder, Property Law (2003).

Bohm, Rechtliche Probleme und Grenzen des tierschutzerischen Aktionismus, in *Harrer/Graf* 47.

Darmann, Pets and Animal Friends. Uber Nahe und Ferne von Menschen und Tieren, in *Krason/Willmitzer* 12.

F. Bydlinski, Der Ersatz ideellen Schaden als sachliches und methodisches Problem (Teil I/II), JBl 1965, 173, 237.

P. Bydlinski/Perner/Spitzer (eds.), Kommentar zum ABGB, KBB[7] (2023).

Fenyves/Kerschner/Vonkilch (eds.), 3rd edition of the commentary on the General Civil Code founded by Dr Heinrich Klang §§ 1-43 (2014); §§ 44-136 (2021); §§ 285-352 (2011); §§ 1331-1341 (2023).

Gerdes, Mourning the loss of a pet from a psychosomatic-psychotherapeutic perspective, in *Schmitt/Kunzmann* 124.

Geroldinger, The wilful legal dispute (2017).

Harrer/Graf (eds.), Tierschutz und Recht (1994).

Hasenohrl, Das oesterreichische Obligationenrecht II[2] (1899).

Hinteregger, Family Law[10] (2022).

Hinteregger, Trauerschmerzengeld und der Anspruch auf immateriellen Schadenersatz im osterreichischen Recht, in FS Danzl 71.

Huber, comment on 6 Ob 177/19a, ZVR 2021, 398.

Huber/Neumayr/Reisinger (eds.), Festschrift Karl-Heinz Danzl on his 65th birthday (2017).

Julius/Beetz/Kotrschal/Turner/Uvnas-Moberg, Attachment to animals. Psychological and neurobiological foundations of animal-assisted interventions (2014).

Kadecka, Bosheit und Mutwille, GZ 1909, 242.

Karner, comment on OGH 16 May 2001, 2 Ob 84/01v, ZVR 2001, 287.

Karner, Der Ersatz ideeller Schaden bei Korperverletzung (1999).

Karner, Turnaround in case law for shock and remote damage to third parties? ZVR 1998, 182.

Karner, Zur Ersatzfahigkeit von Schock- und Trauerschaden - eine Bilanz, in FS Danzl 87.

Kerschner (ed.), Schmerzgeld. Kommentar und Judikatur^2 (2020).

Kitchenham, animal best friends. Love knows no boundaries (2021).

Klang (ed.), Kommentar zum Allgemeinen burgerlichen Gesetzbuch VI^2 (1951).

Kletecka/Schauer (eds.), ABGB-ON. Commentary on the General Civil Code (last update: 2023).

Koziol, Osterreichisches Haftpflichtrecht I^4 (2020); II^3 (2018).

Kramer, Schockschaden mit Krankheitswert - noch offene Fragen? in FS Koziol 743.

Krason/Willmitzer (ed.), Tierisch beste Freunde. Uber Haustiere und ihre Menschen (2017).

Mahr, Animal-assisted interventions. Integration of animals in inpatient child and youth welfare facilities in Austria (2023) (Master's thesis Graz, available at https://unipub.uni-graz.at/urn/urn:nbn:at:at-ubg:1-187742 or urn:nbn:at:at-ubg:1- 187742).

Mayer-Maly, Gedanken zum Ersatz immaterieller Schaden, DRdA 1965, 56.

Muhlehner, Die Tierhaltung in Bestandsobjekten - Zulassigkeit der Haltung versus vertragliche Beschränkung (2023) (Diploma thesis Linz, available at https://epub.jku.at/obvulihs/id/8880297 or urn:nbn:at:at-ubl:1-63847).

Nippel, Erlauterung des allgemeinen burgerlichen Gesetzbuches fur die gesammten deutschen Lander der osterreichischen Monarchie, mit besonderer Berucksichtigung des practischen Bedurfnisses VIII/1 (1835).

Ofner (ed.), Der Ur-Entwurf und die Berathungs-Protokolle des Oesterreichischen Allgemeinen burgerlichen Gesetzbuches II (1889).

Perner/Spitzer/Kodek, Burgerliches Recht[7] (2022).

Pletzer, Once again: Ban on keeping cats and dogs in the form rental agreement? wobl 2013, 249.

Reischauer, comment on 4 Ob 208/17t, JBl 2018, 660.

Riedler, Zivilrecht IV Schuldrecht Besonderer Teil - Gesetzliche Schuldverhaltnisse[6] (2022).

Rummel (ed.), Kommentar zum Allgemeinen burgerlichen Gesetzbuch I[3] (2000); II[3] (sub-volumes: 2004 and 2007, rdb.at).

Rummel/Lukas (eds.), Commentary on the General Civil Code §§ 285-446 (2016).

Schickmair, Dogmatik des Schmerzengeldrechts, in *Kerschner* 17.

Schmitt/Kunzmann (eds.), Not only your pet dies. Stories and research on mourning for pets (2020).

Schoditsch, Die schadenersatzrechtliche "Kemfamilie" im Licht des Art 8 MRK, OJZ 2024, 283.

Schwimann (ed.), ABGB Praxiskommentar VI[3] (2006).

Schwimann/Kodek (eds.), ABGB Praxiskommentar VI[4] (2016).

Schwimann/Neumayr (eds.), ABGB Taschenkommentar[5] (2020).

Spitzer, Compensation for data protection violations. At the same time, comments on the state of discussion on compensation for non-material damage, OJZ 2019, 629.

Strasser, Der immaterielle Schaden im osterreichischen Recht (1964).

Straub/Biller-Bomhardt, Compensation for shock damage in the event of injury or death of an animal, NJW 2021, 118.

Stubenrauch (Begr), Commentar zum osterreichischen allgemeinen burgerlichen

Gesetzbuche II[8] (1903) (ed. by *Schuster von Bonnott/Schreiber*).

Tuma-Koch, The special status of animals in civil law (2021).

Wagner,   Anm zu 2 Ob 142/20a, IUR-Newsletter 4/2021, 10, https://www.jku.at/fileadmin/gruppen/147/PDF/Newsletter/IUR-NL_2021-04.pdf (retrieved on 01/06/2024).

Wagner, Zivilrecht VI Familienrecht[5] (2022).

Wild/Weichbold, The compensability of non-material damage as a result of the confusion of children after birth. A discussion of the decision of the Supreme Court of 22 March 2018, 4 Ob 208/17t, iFamZ 2018, 272.

Wischermann, Between "Cattle" and "Friend". Historische Annaherungen an das Selbst eines Tieres, in *Krason/Willmitzer* 49.

Zeiller, Commentar uber das allgemeine burgerliche Gesetzbuch fur die gesammten Deutschen Erblander der Oesterreichischen Monarchie III/2 (1812).

https://de.statista.com/statistik/daten/studie/1167139/umfrage/verhaeltnis-von-pet-owners-to-their-pets/

(retrieved on 01/06/2024).

https://de.statista.com/statistik/daten/studie/1336090/umfrage/umfrage-zur-importance-of-pets-in-austria/

(retrieved on 01/06/2024).

https://www.gfk.com/de/insights/haustiere-im-internationalen-vergleich

(accessed on 01/06/2024).

https://www.ots.at/presseaussendung/OTS_20220928_OTS0110/heimtierstudie-in- every-other-household-has-a-pet-picture

(retrieved on 01/06/2024).

https://www.sueddeutsche.de/leben/tiere-tierbestattungen-werden-immer-beliebter- dpa.urn-newsml-dpa-com-20090101-200212-99-881824

(retrieved on 01/06/2024).

https://www.zza-online.de/branche/branche/article/tierische-familienmitglieder-wie- leben-die-oesterreicher-mit-ihren-heimtieren.html

(retrieved on 01/06/2024).

Legal provisions

The following is a selection of standards central to the subject matter for quick reference.[219]

<u>§ 16 ABGB</u>

Every human being has inherent rights, which are already obvious through reason, and is therefore to be regarded as a person. Slavery or serfdom, and the exercise of any power relating thereto, is not permitted in these countries.

<u>§ 285 ABGB</u>

Everything that is distinct from the person and serves the use of people is called a thing in the legal sense.

<u>§ Section 285a ABGB</u>

Animals are not property; they are protected by special laws. The regulations applicable to property are only applicable to animals insofar as no deviating regulations exist.

<u>§ 1293 ABGB</u>

Damage means any disadvantage that has been inflicted on someone[220] in terms of property, rights or person. This differs from the loss of profit that someone has to expect in the normal course of events.

<u>§ 1295 ABGB</u>

Para. 1: Every person is entitled to demand compensation from the damaging party for the damage caused to him through his fault; the damage may have been caused by a breach of a contractual obligation or without reference to a contract.

Para. 2: A person who intentionally causes damage in a manner contrary to morality is also liable for it, but if this was done in exercise of a right, only if the exercise of the right was obviously intended to harm the other person.

<u>§ 1323 ABGB</u>

In order to provide compensation for damage caused, everything must be restored to its previous state or, if this is not feasible, the value of the treasure must be compensated. If the compensation relates only to the damage suffered, it is actually called indemnification; but if it also extends to the loss of profit and the redemption of the offence caused, it is called full satisfaction.

<u>§ 1324 ABGB</u>

---

[219] The spelling of individual words has been adapted to the current spelling.
[220] In the original: "someone".

In the case of damage caused by malicious intent or conspicuous carelessness, the injured party is entitled to full satisfaction; in other cases, however, he is only entitled to demand actual indemnification. Hereafter, in cases where the law uses the general term: compensation, it is to be judged what kind of compensation is to be paid.

§ 1325 ABGB

Anyone who injures someone's body shall pay the injured person's medical expenses, compensate him for the loss of earnings or, if the injured person becomes unable to earn a living, also for the future loss of earnings; and, on request, shall also pay him compensation for pain and suffering commensurate with the circumstances.

§ 1327 ABGB

If death results from a physical injury, not only must all costs be compensated, but also the surviving dependants, for whose maintenance the deceased had to provide according to the law, must be compensated for what they have lost as a result.

§ 1331 ABGB

If a person suffers damage to his property intentionally or through the conspicuous carelessness of another person, he is also entitled to claim the loss of profit and, if the damage was caused by an act prohibited by a criminal law or by wilful misconduct or gloating, the value of the particular preference.

§ 1332 ABGB

Damage caused by a lesser degree of negligence or negligence shall be compensated according to the common value of the object at the time of the damage.

§ 1332a ABGB

If an animal is injured, the costs actually incurred for healing or attempted healing shall be charged even if they exceed the value of the animal, provided that a reasonable animal owner in the position of the injured party would have incurred these costs.

Art 8 ECHR

Para. 1: Everyone has the right to respect for his private and family life, his home and his correspondence. Additional information about the author

The author researches and teaches in the field of civil law as a whole; numerous publications on tort law.

Selection of recent publications:

Aigner, Zur Auslegung von AGB und zur Bedeutung der Vertrauensstheorie, VbR 2023/40, 50.

Aigner, The Civil Law Settlement. A comprehensive analysis of the substantive settlement agreement pursuant to §§ 1380 ff ABGB including novation and acknowledgement (2022).

Aigner, On the protective purpose of the prohibition to cross restricted traffic lines, comment on 2 Ob 57/22d, ZVR 2022/158, 345.

Apathy/Aigner/Wolkerstorfer, Zivilrecht VII Erbrecht[7] (2022).

Kerschner/Wagner/Aigner, Civil Law VIII Private International Law[6] (2022).